George Washington

FOUNDING FATHER

D0003830

By Laurence Santrey and JoAnn Early Macken
Illustrated by William Ostrowsey

SCHOLASTIC INC.
New York   Toronto   London   Auckland   Sydney
Mexico City   New Delhi   Hong Kong   Buenos Aires

ISBN-13: 978-0-439-88004-6
ISBN-10: 0-439-88004-1

12 11 10 9 8 7 6 5 4 3 2 1   7 8 9 10 11 12/0

Printed in the U.S.A.
First printing, January 2007

CONTENTS

CHAPTER 1:
Three Early Homes

Although many stories have been told about George Washington's early life, not much is known for sure.

Many people have heard the famous tale about his chopping down a cherry tree. In the story, George was about six years old. Someone had given him a hatchet as a gift. He was, "constantly going about chopping everything that came in his way." One day, he chopped his father's favorite cherry tree. His father asked who did it. "I can't tell a lie, Pa;

you know I can't tell a lie," the boy replied. "I did cut it with my hatchet." His father was thrilled that George told him the truth.

That story was made up for a biography by Mason Locke Weems that was first published in 1800. Weems claimed that a relative of the Washington family told him the story, but it's likely that he made that up, too.

In another story, George threw a coin all the way across the Potomac River. That tale was also invented. The stories were meant to show George's honesty and strength.

George was born on February 22, 1732. His parents, Augustine and Mary Washington, lived on a tobacco farm in Pope's Creek, Virginia. His father also had an iron mine. Their plain wooden house had four rooms, a front porch, and a long, sloping roof.

The Washingtons had lived on the land for many years. George's great-grandfather, John, had sailed from England in 1657. He settled in Virginia in 1658 after marrying Anne Pope.

In those days, tobacco was used as money, and much of it was exported. Many people were needed all year long to grow tobacco. More than fifty slaves worked in the fields and the house. They cleared the fields, planted seeds, and pulled weeds. They hung the grown plants to dry and packed them in huge barrels. Slaves also may have made the barrels, taken care of animals, and worked in the house as cooks and maids.

In 1735, when George was three, the family moved about forty miles to Little Hunting Creek. Their new, larger home on a hill overlooked the wide, beautiful Potomac River. Little Hunting Creek

was a perfect place for a boy who loved adventure. George could roam in the woods with his father, looking for animals and birds. Not far away was the bubbling creek, filled with fish to be caught. Virginia was a fine place to grow up.

The new, two-story home of the Washingtons was fine, but simple. Downstairs, a hall ran through the center of the house from the front door to the back door. On each side of this hall were two rooms—a dining room, a den, and two parlors. Upstairs were another hall and three bedrooms. All the rooms were small.

Around the main house stood several one-room buildings, most likely including a kitchen, an outhouse, and a barn.

The Washingtons lived at Little Hunting Creek for three happy, peaceful years. George learned to ride a pony. He played with his little sister, Betty, and his baby brother, Samuel. Two more brothers, John and Charles, were born during those years. No neighbors lived nearby, so the children played with each other.

When George was seven, the family moved again. Ferry Farm, their new home, was across the Rappahannock River from the small town of Fredericksburg, Virginia. The house was lit by candles

and heated by fireplaces. It had six rooms and thirteen beds. The farm was named for a ferry that crossed the river. The Washingtons sometimes allowed ferry travelers to sleep in their extra beds.

Most of the family's food came from crops that were grown or animals that were raised on the farm. Most of their dishes and utensils were made of wood. They were proud to own twenty-six silver spoons!

CHAPTER 2:
Learning Lessons

In those days, most children studied at home. They learned reading, writing, and simple arithmetic. From Ferry Farm, George may have taken the ferry across the river to a one-room school in Fredericksburg.

George was good at math. Numbers made sense to him. Two and two always added up to four. Six times five was always thirty. When he grew older, George studied Latin, astronomy, and geometry.

But spelling was never easy for George. He thought it was silly that the word *through* didn't rhyme with the word *rough*. He believed that *through* should be spelled *threw* and that *rough* should be spelled *ruff*.

"Words should look the way they sound," he said.

"There is sense in what you say, George," his teacher said. "But you must learn to spell as we all do. If you wish to be thought of as a gentleman, you must spell correctly and write with a fine, clear hand."

George tried to do as his teacher suggested. "Seek the words you need in the books in your father's library," he said. "Read and try to remember everything you read."

When George could not spell a word, he looked through his father's books.

Sometimes he had to read for hours before the word turned up. There were no dictionaries, so George had no easy way to look up the spelling or meaning of a new word.

George had two older half-brothers, Lawrence and Austin, who were the sons of Mr. Washington and his first wife, Jane Butler Washington. The brothers had years of schooling in England, and George wanted to be a gentleman like they were. If spelling and good penmanship were needed, then he would work hard to improve his. He practiced his writing over and over, trying to make the letters round and smooth.

George wanted practical knowledge and good manners. As with spelling, he often turned to books for help. One book he studied was *The Young Man's Companion*. It explained how to measure

land and lumber, how to plant trees, how to make ink, and how to write letters. Another book was called *Rules of Civility and Decent Behavior in Company and Conversation*. It included such rules as "Talk not with meat in your mouth" and "Cleanse not your teeth with the tablecloth." When he was about fifteen, George copied all 110 rules of good manners into a notebook. He always tried to live by them. Some rules were easier than others.

CHAPTER 3:
George's Hero

George had other interests besides books and good manners. He was a tall, strong, healthy boy who was good at sports. From the day he first sat on a pony, George loved to ride. He rode both bareback and with a saddle. No horse was too spirited for him, no stream was too wide to jump, and no fence was too high to clear. He could ride for hours and hours. Many years later, Thomas Jefferson called George Washington the finest horseman he had ever seen.

Young George was a fine marksman, too. Learning to shoot was not just for fun. George and his father found deer, ducks, squirrels, rabbits, and grouse on their land. The wild animals they bagged were food for the family.

George excelled at every sport he tried. He was the best wrestler and the fastest runner of the boys his age in the area.

When it came to pole vaulting and "throwing the bar"—like throwing the javelin today—not even the older boys could beat George.

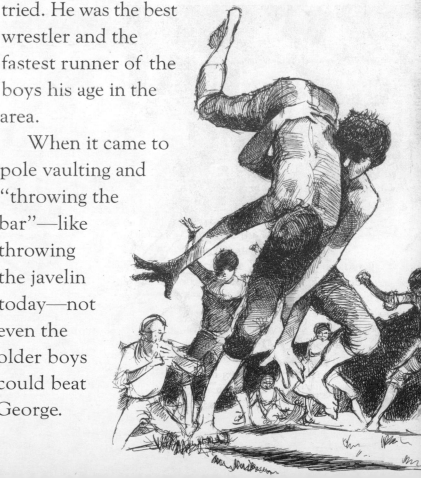

Living on the river gave George plenty of chances for fishing, swimming, and boating. He often rode the ferry across to Fredericksburg to see the sights. He explored the wharfs and tobacco warehouses, the courthouse and the quarry.

When George was ten, his two half-brothers, Lawrence and Austin, returned home from living abroad. Austin arrived from England, where he had finished his schooling.

Lawrence had been on the Caribbean Sea. He had served as an officer in the Virginia Regiment of the British Army under Admiral Edward Vernon. They had taken part in an attempt to capture the city of Cartagena from Spain. The British were badly beaten. Only one-third of the colonial volunteers came back. Lawrence, with his gleaming medals and sword, became George's hero.

CHAPTER 4:
A Change in Plans

In the spring of 1743, when George was eleven, his father died. Augustine Washington left a great deal of property to his family. Lawrence, the oldest son, was given the two thousand five hundred-acre estate on Little Hunting Creek. Besides the land, he inherited a mill, cattle, furniture, and some slaves.

Austin, the second oldest, got the farm at Pope's Creek. He also inherited twenty-five head of cattle, forty hogs, twenty sheep, and some more slaves.

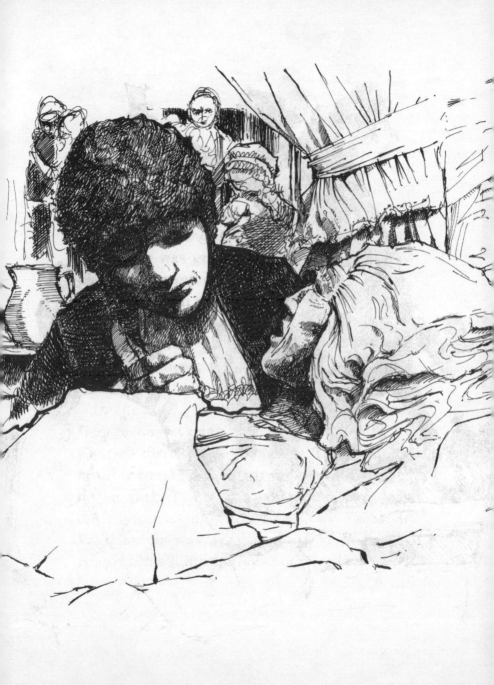

George was given Ferry Farm, with its cattle, sheep, hogs, and horses, and ten slaves. George's younger brothers, Samuel, John, and Charles, all received smaller farms of six or seven hundred acres. Betty, the only daughter, was given two slaves and a large sum of money— four hundred pounds—when she turned eighteen.

An inventory taken that year shows the family's other property. Besides their furniture, it lists a fireplace set, tablecloths, and napkins. The list includes a watch, a sword, eleven china plates, and a looking glass. The family also owned sixteen pairs of sheets and seventeen pillowcases.

Mrs. Washington was left in charge of the property willed to George and his younger brothers. She was to look after the farms until the boys turned twenty-one. She lived with the family at Ferry Farm.

George expected to go to school in England as his older half-brothers had. But when his father died, George lost his chance. There was not enough money. For the rest of George's life, he was sorry he had not gotten a better education.

After George's father died, his mother often left him in charge of his younger brothers and sister. His mother was hard to please. She found fault with nearly everything he did. She grumbled and complained, and they often disagreed. Whenever he could, George left home and stayed with Lawrence or Austin.

CHAPTER 5:
Becoming a Gentleman

Soon after his father's death, George went to visit Lawrence at Little Hunting Creek. George still had a lot to learn about running a farm, and Lawrence offered to teach him. Lawrence took him into the fields and showed him how tobacco was planted, tended, and harvested. He introduced George to all the important people living nearby. He took the boy on fox hunts, to dances and dinner parties, to horse races, and to other social events.

Lawrence enlarged the house at Little Hunting Creek and turned it into a grand mansion. He changed the name to Mount Vernon in honor of Admiral Vernon, under whom Lawrence had served in the British army.

George loved the life he lived there. He admired Lawrence, who was almost like a father to him. He also got along very well with Anne Fairfax Washington, Lawrence's wife. At Mount Vernon, George learned how to dance, how to talk to young ladies, and how to dress well. Learning to be a gentleman mattered as much to George as learning to be a landowner.

George was tall for his age. He had reddish hair, blue eyes, and large hands and feet. During his early teen years, he was busy all the time. When he wasn't at Mount Vernon with Lawrence, he

sometimes stayed with Austin. Then he
might spend two or three months with his
mother. He also visited other relatives in
other parts of Virginia. Since his school
days were over, George filled his time
with travel, new places, and new people—
seeing the world away from Ferry Farm.
Traveling on horseback gave George an
understanding of the land and people that
he could never have gained from books.
These lessons, once learned, were not
forgotten.

George loved adventure, and he longed
to sail at sea. When he was fourteen,
Lawrence arranged a post for him on an
English navy ship, but his mother refused
to let him go. She thought he should
come back to Ferry Farm. After that,
George moved in with Lawrence for good.

Lawrence took him out fishing, riding,
and fox hunting. Austin taught him the

business of running a farm. George didn't mind this at all, since much of it had to do with numbers. He'd always been good at math.

He figured the number of acres to be plowed, how many pounds of tobacco an acre would yield, the taxes, the profits, and the cost of food and clothing. George learned his lessons well. If he had to be a Virginia planter, he wanted to be the best one possible.

CHAPTER 6:
Chance of a Lifetime

In 1747, when he was fifteen, George met Lord Thomas Fairfax at Mount Vernon. He was Anne's father's cousin from England. Lord Fairfax lived in an elegant brick mansion on a nearby estate. He owned more than five million acres of land. He took a liking to the polite, serious young man, and he often invited George to be his houseguest. They rode and hunted together.

One of the things Lord Fairfax liked about George was his willingness to learn from everything he saw, heard, and did. He was always eager to learn new skills and try new things.

In his early teens, George had taught himself how to survey land and draw maps of the areas he measured. He used his father's instruments to measure and mark land boundaries. In those days, people became rich by owning land. A surveyor could find out where the best land was, who owned it, and how much it cost. George thought he could earn money by buying and selling land.

One of George's first maps showed a survey of a turnip field owned by his brother Lawrence. He later made surveys and drew maps of Ferry Farm, Pope's Creek, Mount Vernon, and the town of Belhaven, now known as Alexandria, Virginia.

When Lord Fairfax learned of George's surveying skills, he asked the

teenager to visit him. At dinner, the lord
questioned George about surveying.
George told him how he had learned to
use his father's old surveying tools and
how much he liked the work.

When George was sixteen, Lord
Fairfax invited him to join his cousin,
George William Fairfax, and an
experienced surveyor on a long venture.
They were to chart the lord's land in the
Shenandoah Valley. It was George's first
big chance to earn money. The pay, a
doubloon a day, was worth about seven or
eight dollars at the time—a huge amount.
George had his first chance to see the
wilderness of western Virginia. He had
a real job, and he would be earning
good pay.

CHAPTER 7:
Life in the Wilderness

The surveying party left on March 11, 1748. Spring was in the air. On the first day, they covered forty miles before making camp. In the thirty-three days that followed, sixteen-year-old George had the time of his life. He kept the field notes for the survey. He rode a horse across a river swollen with melting snow. He paddled a canoe forty miles upriver. He got lost in the Blue Ridge Mountains, saw a rattlesnake, and shot wild turkeys for food. He learned how to survive in

the wilderness. He was finally having the adventure he'd always dreamed of.

One of the highlights of the journey was meeting a group of about thirty Native Americans. The two groups camped close to each other in the Shenandoah Valley. In his diary, George described their musical instruments. One drummed on a pot half full of water with deerskins stretched over the top. Another rattled a gourd with a piece of a horse's tail tied to it. George watched with fascination as the Native Americans did a war dance.

George also wrote about the problems and dangers he faced while traveling. He spent one night on a straw bed with only a thin blanket. It was full of fleas and lice! That night, he got up, got dressed, and slept on the floor in his clothes. The group spent the next night in a cozy inn with feather beds and clean sheets.

Most of the time, they slept outside. They kept a fire burning for warmth. One night, the straw they were sleeping on caught fire. One man woke up and warned the others. Another time, a windstorm carried their tent away during the night. In spite of his troubles, George came to love the land and staying outdoors.

As he traveled, George saw how the first people to arrive in a new place could buy land at low prices and sell it to the next settlers for more. His brother Lawrence bought 1,300 acres of the land George had explored. George knew he could do the same if he had money to spend. To get it, he decided to take on more surveying work.

All that George heard and saw and did on this trip changed him. The boy who left Mount Vernon was a budding English gentleman, but the young man who came back was truly an American with a newfound respect for the land of his birth. In those thirty-three days, George discovered forests and rivers and mountains—a new world that reached farther west than the eye could see. He had felt the frontier, and he would never be the same again.

CHAPTER 8:

The Father of Our Country

After George returned from that land surveying trip, Lord Fairfax recommended him for a job as the official surveyor of Culpeper County. George traveled to Williamsburg for training, and then he went to work. For several years, he surveyed land throughout the Blue Ridge Mountains.

With the money he earned, he started buying his own land. He bought a five hundred and fifty-acre plantation in 1748, while he was still only sixteen years old. He bought another plot of land two years later and another two years after that. Before he turned twenty, he owned more than fifteen hundred acres of land.

Around that time, George's brother Lawrence became ill with tuberculosis. At the time, doctors thought a tropical climate would help cure the disease. So Lawrence traveled to the island of Barbados, and George went along. The trip there took more than five weeks.

George's diary from the journey tells of a dolphin and shark that were caught. It describes the violent weather they sailed through. The sailors agreed that there must have been a hurricane nearby. They were glad to feel steady winds, "after near five weeks buffeting and being tossed by a fickle and merciless ocean."

In Barbados, George and Lawrence dined at a fort. They went to a play and

a dinner party. George caught smallpox
at the dinner party and was sick for three
weeks. His face was scarred for the rest
of his life. This trip was the only time
George ever left North America.

The warm climate in Barbados did not
help Lawrence. After they returned home
in 1752, he died.

Lawrence left Mount Vernon to his
young daughter. George was to manage
the property for her, but she died soon

after her father did, and the estate later became George's.

Before he died, Lawrence resigned from the Virginia Militia. George took over his job of overseeing the men. At that time, thirteen British colonies lay along the east coast of North America. The British claimed all the land west to the Appalachian Mountains. The French claimed the land in the Ohio Valley on the other side.

In 1747, the governor of Virginia started giving away land in the Ohio Valley. But the land was not his. To protect their interests, the French began to build forts there. In 1753, the governor sent George to carry a letter to the French commander in the area. The letter told the French to leave.

George rode three hundred miles with an interpreter, a guide, and several servants. He met with the French, who refused to back down. On the way back to Virginia, snow fell. It was so deep that the men left their horses with the interpreter. George and the guide walked the rest of the way.

In 1754, the governor put George Washington in charge of about two hundred men. They were sent to fight the French, who had at least a thousand men and help from Native Americans who lived in the area. When they found a French camp in the woods, Washington's troops killed ten French men. Then they found out that the men had been carrying a message for the governor. This event started the French and Indian War.

Washington and his men built a small fort called Fort Necessity. They built it in an open field, where the French shot right at them. In one day, nearly one-third of the men were killed. Washington saw that it was time to end the fight, surrendered, and took the rest of his men home. At twenty-two, Washington was known as a hero for protecting his men.

A few months later, Washington joined General Edward Braddock in another battle. Braddock marched his men in straight lines along a trail they cleared. Washington told him how the French and Indians fought in the woods, but Braddock would not change his plans. Braddock and many of his men were killed by enemy fighters who hid behind rocks and trees. After that battle, Washington was made commander of the Virginia troops. For several more years, he moved from fort to fort.

In 1759, George Washington retired from the army. He went home to Mount Vernon and married Martha Custis, a widow with a daughter and a son. He got involved in politics.

George stayed at Mount Vernon as often as possible, but it wasn't until the last years of his life that he could spend much time there. Only after serving his country as Commander-in-Chief of the Continental Army and as its first president was George finally free to enjoy the beauty and peace of Mount Vernon.

As George grew older, he came to realize that slavery was wrong. In his will, he said that after he and Martha died, the slaves at Mount Vernon were all to be freed. They were to be taught to read and write. They were to be trained to work or taken care of if they could not work.

One cold morning, George rode out to look over his fields. Within two days, he became so ill that he could hardly speak or swallow. George Washington

died on December 14, 1799. He had
battled heroically for his native land
during the American Revolution. He
became a symbol of strength, honor, and
unshakable faith in freedom. No man
was better suited to be the nation's first
president. And no man is remembered
with more respect.

INDEX

Look for these other exciting
EASY BIOGRAPHIES: